# IDEAS

by
C. C. Paris

illustrated by
Brook Nicol

## Chapters

Harcourt

Orlando   Boston   Dallas   Chicago   San Diego

Visit *The Learning Site!*

www.harcourtschool.com

# Introduction

Have you ever heard someone say, "That's a bright idea?" Perhaps you've seen a lightbulb used to show a person thinking of an idea. It's not by chance that the lightbulb is used to represent good ideas. Thomas Edison's invention has changed the way people everywhere live. Like many other ideas, the lightbulb began as a question that someone wanted to answer. The rest is history.

In this book, you will read about some American inventors who turned simple ideas into products and services that help others. Some of these ideas have solved everyday problems. Others have saved lives and even changed the world. The people who had the ideas were all curious about something. They had an initial idea, and they also had two other important qualities. They worked hard to solve a problem and shared the solution with others.

## Alexander Graham Bell
## The Telephone

Sometimes inventors search for a solution to one problem and find an answer to another. In the 1870s Alexander Graham Bell was looking for a way to help deaf people hear. He set out to design a hearing aid, and began experimenting with electricity. He discovered that different tones changed the strength of an electric current in a wire. Bell built a microphone and receiver that put together the variations and turned them into something that sounded like speech. His invention turned out to be the telephone.

Even Bell's first transmitted message was an accident. In 1876 Bell accidentally spilled some acid on his pants. He called out to his assistant, Thomas A. Watson, "Mr. Watson, come here—I want you." Mr. Watson came running from another floor. He had heard Bell's call for help over the first telephone! Bell's ingenuity had led to an invention that would change the world.

Before the telephone, the telegraph was the most widely used way of sending messages. Unfortunately, you had to know Morse code to use the telegraph. Anybody could use the telephone. It became a sensation.

In 1880, telephones were found in only about 54,000 homes. By 1910, about 7.6 million homes had phones. Telephone use has increased a great deal since then. Like electric lighting, the invention of the telephone is acknowledged as a milestone in modern history.

## U.S. Homes With Telephones 1920-1990

millions

| | 1920 | 1950 | 1990 |
|---|---|---|---|

Alexander Graham Bell became very success-ful because of his invention. Even so, he never forgot about the first problem he wanted to solve. In 1890 he founded the Alexander Graham Bell Association for the Deaf. One of the first people brought to him for help was Helen Keller, who was both blind and deaf. Keller would one day be well known in her own right.

## Lewis Latimer
## Incandescent Lighting

One of the inventors who worked with Thomas Edison to develop the electric lightbulb was a draftsman named Lewis Howard Latimer. Latimer is remembered as a major contributor to the invention of incandescent electric lighting.

Latimer's father was an escaped African American slave. As a young man, Latimer worked for a group of patent attorneys. While employed there, he taught himself drafting. He became so good at drafting that he was given major projects to complete.

In the mid-1870s Latimer provided the drawings for an amazing invention. It was the patent application for the telephone, invented by Alexander Graham Bell.

7

In 1880, a year after Edison produced the first successful electric light, Latimer came up with an idea that made the lightbulb practical for use everywhere. He invented a way to produce carbon filaments. These allowed an

incandescent lightbulb to stay lit for a much longer time. Lightbulbs were soon being used to light homes, stores, and factories everywhere.

Electric lighting was very much in demand. Latimer supervised the installation of electric lights in cities around the world. These cities included London, New York, and Philadelphia.

In 1883 Latimer went to work for Thomas Edison. By 1890 he had published the very first textbook on electric lighting.

## Grace Murray Hopper
## COBOL

Grace Murray grew up in New York City before World War I. As a young girl, she liked to take apart alarm clocks and put them back together to see how they worked. When she was older, she helped her father plan new streets. She was fascinated by all the numbers, angles, curves, and intersections in that type of work. This interest led her to study mathematics in college.

She earned her master's degree from Yale University in 1930. Then she married a man named Vincent Hopper and began teaching at Vassar College.

World War II began. In 1943 Grace Murray Hopper decided she wanted to serve her country. She joined the U.S. Navy. Everyone could see how good she was in mathematics. Before long, she was assigned to work with computers.

Hopper discovered a way to write codes that computers could follow. She hoped that her method would let anyone run a computer.

By 1955 she had finished a code with twenty business commands, such as "count." Her computer program became a model for a new program called COBOL, which stands for Common Business Oriented Language.

In 1985, at the age of 79, Grace Hopper was made a rear admiral by President Ronald Reagan. In 1991, President George Bush acknowledged her achievements, too. He awarded her the National Medal of Technology.

## Jonas Salk
## Polio Vaccine

During the first half of the twentieth century, many children became ill with a terrible disease called polio. Polio is caused by a virus. The children ran high fevers and had terrible back and leg pain. In the worst cases, the children were paralyzed, or unable to stand or walk. Some victims could not even breathe. They needed a special machine to breathe for them.

Jonas Edward Salk was a scientist. He worked hard to find a way to stop polio. He and other scientists spent years experimenting. Finally he came up with a vaccine. Salk believed the vaccine would prevent people from getting polio.

In 1953 Salk announced his idea for the vaccine to the country. He believed so much in the safety of his vaccine that he gave it to himself, his wife, and their three sons. It proved safe.

Salk's brave experiment gave him high visibility. By 1954 the vaccine had been given to more than a million children to see if it would prevent polio. It did! The vaccine was approved for general use in April 1955.

Salk would not accept cash awards for his ideas. However, he received a Congressional gold medal from President Dwight Eisenhower. It was for "great achievement in the field of medicine."

## Albert Einstein
## Lasers

Did you know that the laser price scanners used in stores came from an idea a scientist had more than seventy years ago? Albert Einstein is one of the most famous scientists of all time. He is best known for his formula $E = mc^2$ and other ideas about physics. However, his many inquiries into different areas of science led to the idea for lasers.

Einstein first began his work on lasers in 1917. He found that when light of a certain wavelength hits an atom, the atom gives off light. That light is the same wavelength, which makes it the same color as the light that hit the atom.

Ordinary light has many different wavelengths and spreads in all directions. Einstein suggested that laser light could have rays that are all the same wavelength. They make a very pure color. They also move in the same direction and make a powerful beam.

For many years researchers had a hard time turning Einstein's idea into something useful. However, they kept working on the idea and adding to it. After World War II the microwave oven was invented. It was a direct development of Einstein's first idea. Today lasers are used in many different ways. They are used in compact disc players, eye and brain surgery, and telephone communications.

## Ellen Ochoa
## Space Research

The first Hispanic American female astronaut, Ellen Ochoa, was born in Los Angeles, California. As a child she had no idea that she would ever work in space or become an inventor.

"A lot of my friends decided when they were very young that when they grew up they wanted to become an astronaut," she says. "They decided from a very young age…but for me it was a little different."

What Ochoa had at a young age was a love of learning—especially science. She had other interests as well. She enjoyed music, volleyball, and bicycling. She pursued them all with persistence. She became very good at

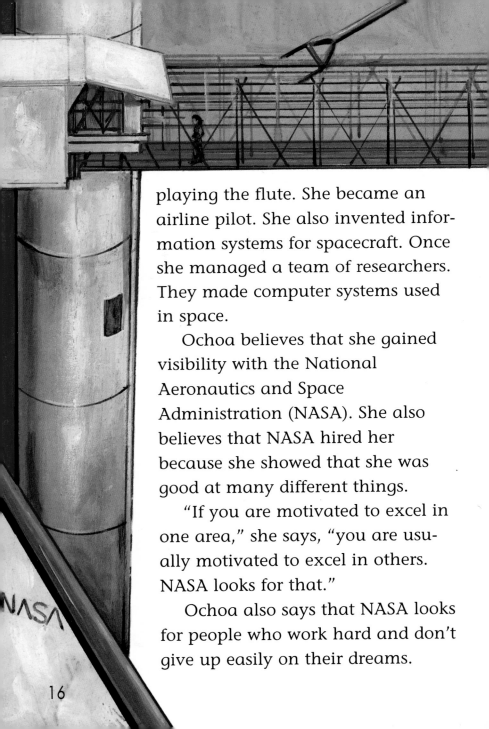

playing the flute. She became an airline pilot. She also invented information systems for spacecraft. Once she managed a team of researchers. They made computer systems used in space.

Ochoa believes that she gained visibility with the National Aeronautics and Space Administration (NASA). She also believes that NASA hired her because she showed that she was good at many different things.

"If you are motivated to excel in one area," she says, "you are usually motivated to excel in others. NASA looks for that."

Ochoa also says that NASA looks for people who work hard and don't give up easily on their dreams.